D1436266

52 THINGS TO DO
WHILE YOU POO

THE SPORTS EDITION

SUMMERSDALE PUBLISHERS LTD
46 WEST STREET
CHICHESTER
WEST SUSSEX
PO19 1RP
UK

WWW.SUMMERSDALE.COM
PRINTED AND BOUND IN CHINA
ISBN: 978-1-78685-268-7

SUBSTANTIAL DISCOUNTS ON BULK QUANTITIES OF SUMMERSDALE BOOKS ARE AVAILABLE TO CORPORATIONS, PROFESSIONAL ASSOCIATIONS AND OTHER ORGANISATIONS. FOR DETAILS CONTACT GENERAL ENQUIRIES BY TELEPHONE: +44 (0) 1243 771107 OR EMAIL: ENQUIRIES@SUMMERSDALE.COM

THIS PAIR ONLY APPEARS ONCE
ON THE OPPOSITE PAGE

KNOW
SPORT?

WHICH SPORT IS PLAYED
ON THE BIGGEST PITCH?

A) BASEBALL

B) POLO

C) GAELIC FOOTBALL

WHAT IS THE HIGHEST POSSIBLE BREAK IN SNOOKER?

A) 147

B) 155

C) 161

HIT THE GREEN – NOT THE TREES!

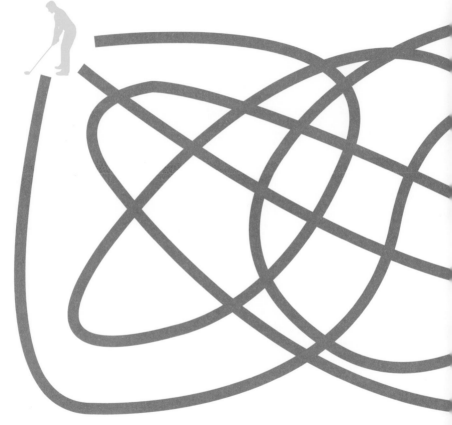

52 THINGS TO DO WHILE YOU POO

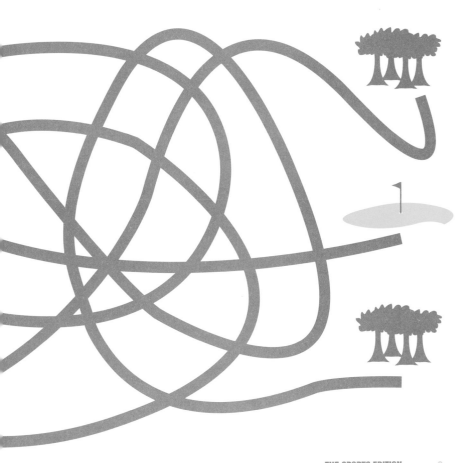

FOOTBALL

RUGBY

CRICKET

GOLF

TENNIS

CYCLING

BADMINTON

SQUASH

NETBALL

HOCKEY

S F Q U N A H S H M
H O C K E Y S V T N
D O S A T C A C E B
Y T F G B H U R N C
B B L K A J Q I N Y
G A M N L B S C I C
U L G O L F V K S L
R L R E W Q C E C I
G B A D M I N T O N
T Y U I O P S Q U G

WHICH ITALIAN FOOTBALL TEAM IS NICKNAMED 'THE OLD LADY'?

A) A.C. MILAN

B) ROMA

C) JUVENTUS

IF EVERY BATSMAN IN A CRICKET TEAM GETS BOWLED OUT FIRST BALL, WHICH NUMBER BATSMAN REMAINS 'NOT OUT'?

A) BATSMAN NUMBER 3

B) BATSMAN NUMBER 8

C) BATSMAN NUMBER 11

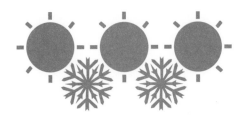

WHICH CITY IS THE FIRST TO BE AWARDED BOTH THE SUMMER OLYMPICS (2008) AND THE WINTER OLYMPICS (2022)?

A) LOS ANGELES

B) BEIJING

C) SYDNEY

**IN 1963 HE BECAME THE YOUNGEST
PERSON TO WIN THE MASTERS.
IN 1986 HE BECAME THE OLDEST.
WHO WAS THIS GOLFING LEGEND?**

A) ARNOLD PALMER

B) GARY PLAYER

C) JACK NICKLAUS

C_____ P___ CELTIC

I____ S_____ RANGERS

E____ P___ BLACKBURN ROVERS

C___ O M_____ S_____ MANCHESTER CITY

O__ T_____ MANCHESTER UNITED

G_____ P___ EVERTON

A_____ LIVERPOOL

M_____ WOLVERHAMPTON WANDERERS

T__ H_____ WEST BROMWICH ALBION

L_____ S_____ SWANSEA CITY

C_____ C__ S_____ CARDIFF CITY

A____ G__ BRISTOL CITY

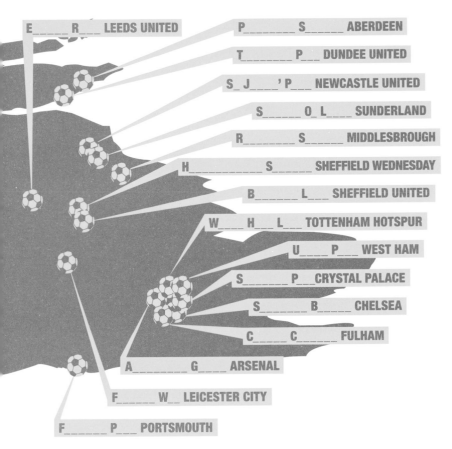

E____ R___ LEEDS UNITED

P_____ S_____ ABERDEEN

T_____ P___ DUNDEE UNITED

S_J____'P____ NEWCASTLE UNITED

S_____O_L____ SUNDERLAND

R_____ S_____ MIDDLESBROUGH

H_____ S_____ SHEFFIELD WEDNESDAY

B_____ L___ SHEFFIELD UNITED

W____H___L___ TOTTENHAM HOTSPUR

U_____P____ WEST HAM

S_____P___ CRYSTAL PALACE

S_____B_____ CHELSEA

C_____C_____ FULHAM

A_____G_____ ARSENAL

F_____W__ LEICESTER CITY

F_____P___ PORTSMOUTH

SPOT THE DIFFERENCE – THERE'S ONLY ONE!

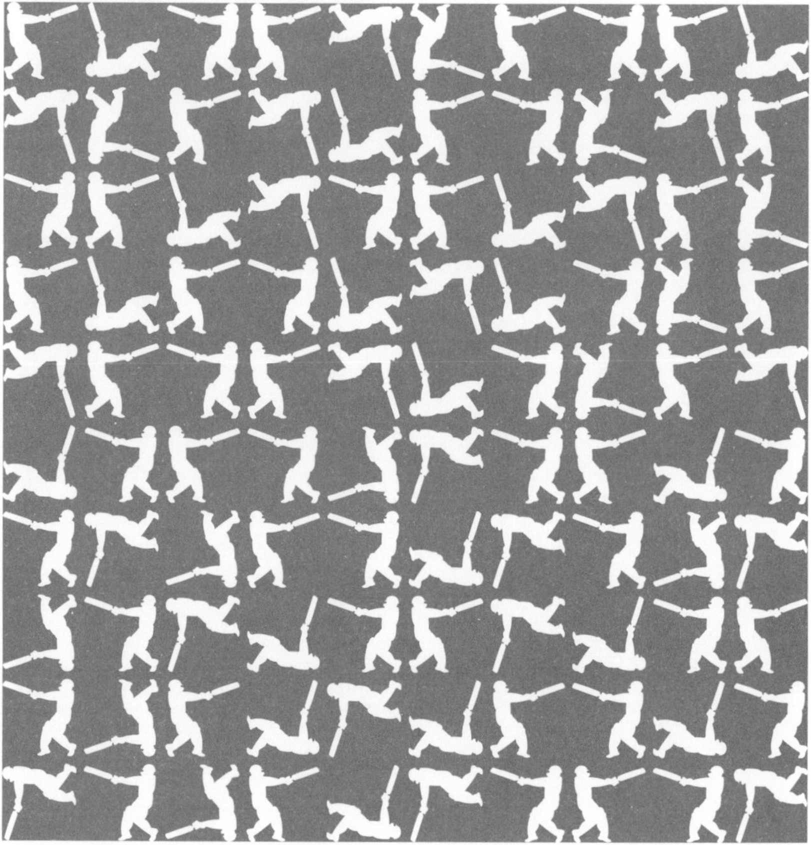

NAME A COUNTRY THAT COMPETES IN
THE OLYMPICS BEGINNING WITH EACH
LETTER OF THE WORD:

O _____

L _____

Y _____

M _____

P _____

I _____

C _____

S _____

WHAT IS THE LOWEST DARTS SCORE YOU <u>CAN'T</u> ACHIEVE WITH A SINGLE DART?

WELCOME TO ANAGRAM RUGBY CLUB – CAN YOU WORK OUT WHO'S ON THE TEAM SHEET?

PROP
SOUTH AFRICA

RUN AT ODDS

1

HOOKER
IRELAND

HOOKED WIT

2

PROP
NEW ZEALAND

CAN LAY HARM

3

LOCK
AUSTRALIA

JEANS HOLE

4

LOCK
SOUTH AFRICA

SHAKE A KIT BOB

5

FLANKER
FRANCE

I HIT DOUR TREASURY

6

NUMBER EIGHT
ITALY

PIE IS A GROSSER

8

FLANKER
SCOTLAND

FAIRLY LANCED

7

RIGHT WING
AUSTRALIA

EVADES
MID CAP

14

FULL-BACK
FRANCE

CLEANERS
BOG

15

LEFT WING
WALES

WE IN A
SMALLISH

11

CENTRE
IRELAND

CLARION
BOLD SIR

13

CENTRE
NEW ZEALAND

AM A
NOUN

12

OUTSIDE-HALF
ENGLAND

WINK JOINS
NYLON

10

SCRUM-HALF
ARGENTINA

TOUCHING
PAS IT

9

WHAT DOES THE CRICKET UMPIRE MEAN? MATCH THE SIGNALS TO THE MEANINGS

LEG-BYE OUT NO BALL SHORT RUN

BOUNDARY 6   BYE   WIDE   NEW BALL

BAGGIO (ROBERTO)
BANKS (GORDON)
BECKHAM (DAVID)
BERGKAMP (DENNIS)
BEST (GEORGE)
CANTONA (ERIC)
PELÉ
ROONEY (WAYNE)
GIGGS (RYAN)
LINEKER (GARY)
MARADONA (DIEGO)
MESSI (LIONEL)

```
N M E S S I L M B C
B Y G F G I G G S H
O E B R N O P M A A
A C R E H K A L N Y
P C K G S H J O O E
A E S D K T D P T N
R G L C H A J K N O
V F E E R B M L A O
A B B A N K S P C R
S D M B A G G I O L
```

THIS PAIR ONLY APPEARS ONCE ON THE OPPOSITE PAGE

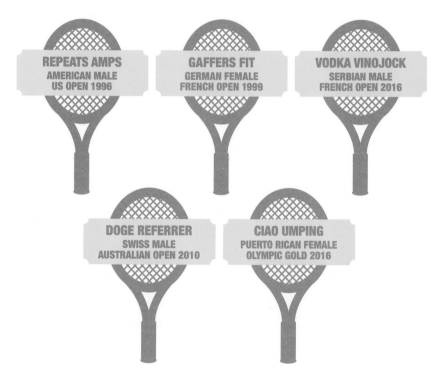

REPEATS AMPS
AMERICAN MALE
US OPEN 1996

GAFFERS FIT
GERMAN FEMALE
FRENCH OPEN 1999

VODKA VINOJOCK
SERBIAN MALE
FRENCH OPEN 2016

DOGE REFERRER
SWISS MALE
AUSTRALIAN OPEN 2010

CIAO UMPING
PUERTO RICAN FEMALE
OLYMPIC GOLD 2016

VARIATION NAVALTRAM
CZECH / AMERICAN FEMALE
WIMBLEDON 1990

CHAP SAT
AUSTRALIAN MALE
WIMBLEDON 1986

SAMOVAR HAPARIA
RUSSIAN FEMALE
US OPEN 2006

CAFETERIA JINNRIP
AMERICAN FEMALE
AUSTRALIAN OPEN 2001

LEAN LAFARAD
SPANISH MALE
OLYMPIC GOLD 2008

MILLENNIUM STADIUM

MY MATCH AGAINST
LEGINGTON LEGBREAKERS
KICKS OFF IN TWO MINUTES.
FIND MY OTHER SHIN PAD!

**WHY DID NASA REFUSE NEIL
ARMSTRONG'S REQUEST TO TAKE
A FOOTBALL TO THE MOON?**

A) IT WAS TOO CUMBERSOME

B) IT WAS A NON-ESSENTIAL ITEM

C) IT WAS UN-AMERICAN

HOW LONG DID ROGER BANNISTER HOLD THE WORLD RECORD FOR THE FASTEST MILE?

A) 46 DAYS

B) 46 WEEKS

C) 46 YEARS

WHAT DO THE RUGBY REF AND ASSISTANT MEAN? MATCH THE SIGNALS TO THE MEANINGS

KNOCK ON   BALL NOT RELEASED   FREE KICK   PENALTY

LINE-OUT THROW NOT STRAIGHT **TRY** **OBSTRUCTION** **FORWARD PASS**

THIS PAIR ONLY APPEARS ONCE
ON THE OPPOSITE PAGE

WELCOME TO THE CRICKET ANAGRAM HALL OF FAME – CAN YOU WORK OUT WHO'S MADE IT?

NORMAL BAND DAD

AUSTRALIAN
BATSMAN

GRASSY ROBE

WEST INDIAN
ALL-ROUNDER

RAINS VIVID ARCH

WEST INDIAN
BATSMAN

HI RANK MAN

PAKISTANI
ALL-ROUNDER

HIM ONA BAT

ENGLISH
ALL-ROUNDER

ENILL LINSEED

AUSTRALIAN
FAST BOWLER

ELS JAIL QUACKS

**SOUTH AFRICAN
ALL-ROUNDER**

DIVED AND A JAM

**PAKISTANI
BATSMAN**

HE EARNS WAN

**AUSTRALIAN
SPIN BOWLER**

MASK WAR AIM

**PAKISTANI
ALL-ROUNDER**

RAN AIR LAB

**WEST INDIAN
BATSMAN**

TRICKING PONY

**AUSTRALIAN
BATSMAN**

SPOT THE DIFFERENCE – THERE'S ONLY ONE!

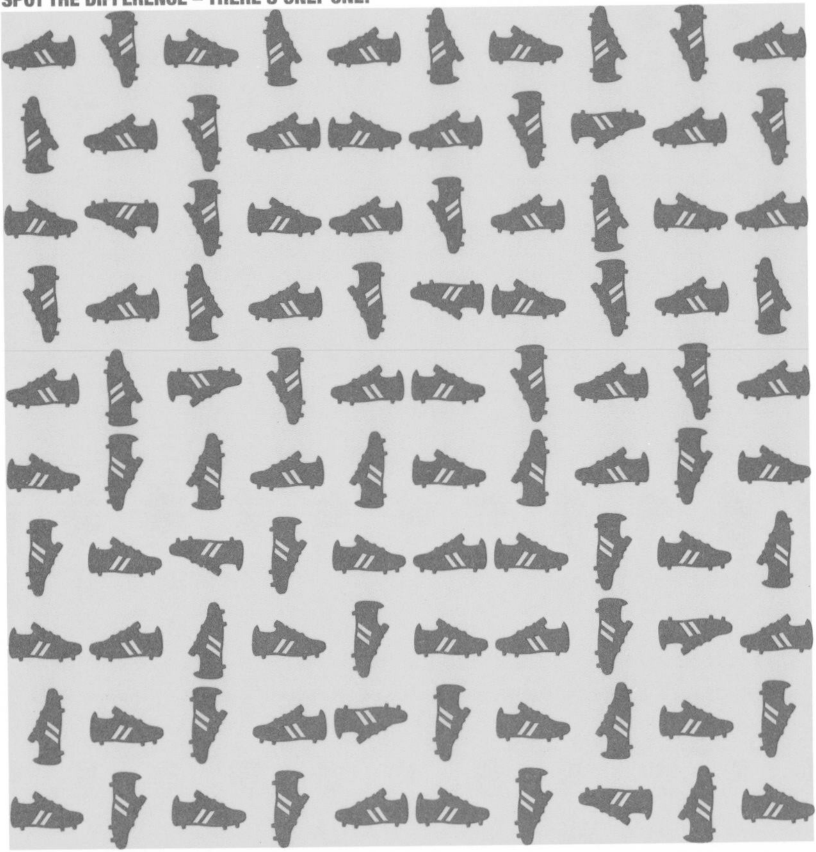

WHICH IS THE WORLD'S OLDEST SURVIVING RUGBY CLUB?

A) BLACKHEATH FOOTBALL CLUB

B) DUBLIN UNIVERSITY FOOTBALL CLUB

C) HARLEQUINS FOOTBALL CLUB

WHICH OF THESE COUNTRIES HAS RUGBY LEAGUE AS ITS NATIONAL SPORT?

A) NEW ZEALAND

B) MADAGASCAR

C) PAPUA NEW GUINEA

WHAT OCCURS ONCE IN

HOCKEY

TWICE IN

FOOTBALL

BUT NEVER IN

BASEBALL

THE BATSMAN'S EDGED IT AND YOU'RE AT SLIP!

**IN WHICH SPORT DO WINNERS
MOVE BACKWARDS AND LOSERS
MOVE FORWARDS?**

WHICH BRITISH FIELD ATHLETE COMPETED AT SIX OLYMPIC GAMES?

A) TESSA SANDERSON

B) FATIMA WHITBREAD

C) DALEY THOMPSON

I'VE LOST MY RUGBY BALL!

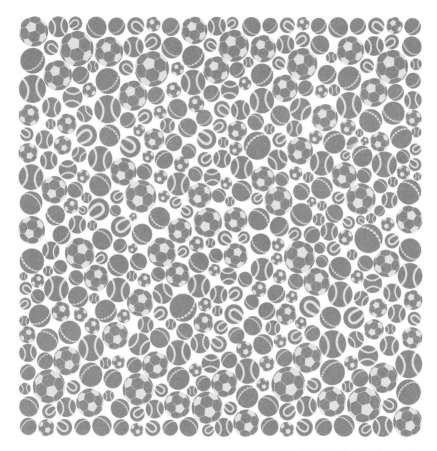

IN 1981 MUHAMMAD ALI RETIRED FROM
BOXING – WHAT WAS HIS CAREER RECORD?

A) 55 WINS, 5 DEFEATS

B) 59 WINS, 1 DEFEATS

C) 60 WINS, 0 DEFEATS

**SERGEY BUBKA AND RENAUD LAVILLENIE
ARE MEMBERS OF WHICH EXCLUSIVE
6-METRE-HIGH CLUB?**

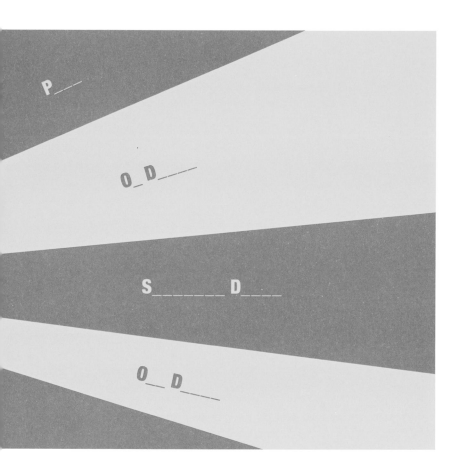

P___

O_ D_____

S_____ D_____

O__ D_____

THIS PAIR ONLY APPEARS ONCE
ON THE OPPOSITE PAGE

WHAT IS THE REGULATION HEIGHT OF A BASKETBALL HOOP?

A) 9 FT / 2.74 M

B) 10 FT / 3.05 M

C) 11 FT / 3.35 M

WHAT IS THE REGULATION HEIGHT OF A NETBALL HOOP?

A) 9 FT / 2.74 M

B) 10 FT / 3.05 M

C) 11 FT / 3.35 M

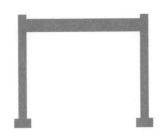

HOW MANY HURDLES ARE THERE IN THE MEN'S 110 M HURDLES EVENT?

A) 9

B) 10

C) 11

CURLING ORIGINATED IN THE SIXTEENTH CENTURY AND WAS PLAYED ON FROZEN PONDS AND LAKES – IN WHICH COUNTRY?

A) SCOTLAND

B) NEW ZEALAND

C) CANADA

52 THINGS TO DO WHILE YOU POO

IN 2010, AT WIMBLEDON, JOHN ISNER AND NICOLAS MAHUT BROKE THE RECORD FOR THE LONGEST TENNIS MATCH. WAS IT:

A) 11 HOURS AND 5 MINUTES

B) 7 HOURS AND 24 MINUTES

C) 9 HOURS AND 8 MINUTES

AT THE MOSCOW 1980 OLYMPICS, WHAT WAS SIGNIFICANT ABOUT THE GOLD- AND SILVER-MEDAL-WINNING ROWING TEAMS IN THE MEN'S COXLESS PAIRS?

A) BOTH PAIRS WERE FATHER AND SON

B) BOTH PAIRS WERE BROTHERS

C) BOTH PAIRS WERE IDENTICAL TWINS

WELCOME TO THE FOOTBALL ANAGRAM TROPHY CABINET – CAN YOU WORK OUT THE CUP WINNERS?

CYNIC TRY VOTE

FA CUP
WINNERS 1987

NEED BARE

UEFA CUP
WINNERS 1983

ENTRY WAS GEM

WORLD CUP
WINNERS 1990

RED MEN BREWER

UEFA CUP
WINNERS 1992

THE TANTRUM PHOTOS

FA CUP
WINNERS 1967

MINI RENTAL

COPPA ITALIA
WINNERS 2011

VISA
CRY TOO

AFRICA CUP OF NATIONS
WINNERS 1992

DIRT AIM
LOCATED

COPA DEL REY
WINNERS 2013

UNEDITED
NUDE

SCOTTISH CUP
WINNERS 2010

NEAR
GIANT

WORLD CUP
WINNERS 1986

ANT
SWAYS ICE

WELSH CUP
WINNERS 1991

THE
WAILING ACT

FA CUP
WINNERS 2013

**WHICH COUNTRY'S PARALYMPIC
BASKETBALL TEAM WON GOLD IN 2000
BUT WERE LATER DISQUALIFIED
WHEN MOST OF THE TEAM WERE FOUND
NOT TO BE DISABLED?**

A FIELD POLO MATCH IS DIVIDED INTO TIME PERIODS CALLED WHAT?

A) CHUCKS

B) CHICKENS

C) CHUKKAS

THIS PAIR ONLY APPEARS ONCE
ON THE OPPOSITE PAGE

CHARLENE, PRINCESS OF MONACO, COMPETED AT THE 2000 SYDNEY OLYMPICS – WHICH COUNTRY DID SHE REPRESENT AND IN WHAT EVENT?

A) CANADA, INDIVIDUAL DRESSAGE

B) SOUTH AFRICA, 4×100 M MEDLEY RELAY

C) FRANCE, FENCING – INDIVIDUAL SABRE

WHAT IS TIGER WOODS' REAL FIRST NAME?

A) ELDRICK

B) RODERICK

C) BALDRICK

? ? ? ?

WHAT SPORT HAS FOUR LETTERS, IS PLAYED ALL AROUND THE WORLD, AND BEGINS WITH A 'T'?

YOU NEED A RUB DOWN – GET TO THE PHYSIO!

PHYSIO

EDEN (PARK) (NEW ZEALAND)
THE OVAL (ENGLAND)
SABINA (PARK) (JAMAICA)
LORD'S (ENGLAND)
CARISBROOK (NEW ZEALAND)
ELLIS (PARK) (SOUTH AFRICA)
SOPHIA (GARDENS) (WALES)
SAHARA (PARK) (SOUTH AFRICA)
EDGBASTON (ENGLAND)
GREEN (PARK) (INDIA)

E	A	Y	L	A	S	I	B	P	K
L	H	G	F	I	E	E	D	O	C
L	O	G	I	H	D	D	O	J	L
I	P	R	O	P	G	R	E	N	M
S	A	E	D	O	B	T	U	N	V
R	N	E	S	S	A	H	A	R	A
O	I	N	I	I	S	E	A	Y	W
U	B	R	F	I	T	O	N	J	O
R	A	T	H	E	O	V	A	L	N
C	S	T	E	I	N	H	G	S	E

WE CAN'T SCRUMMAGE WITHOUT OUR TIGHT-HEAD PROP! CAN YOU FIND HIM?

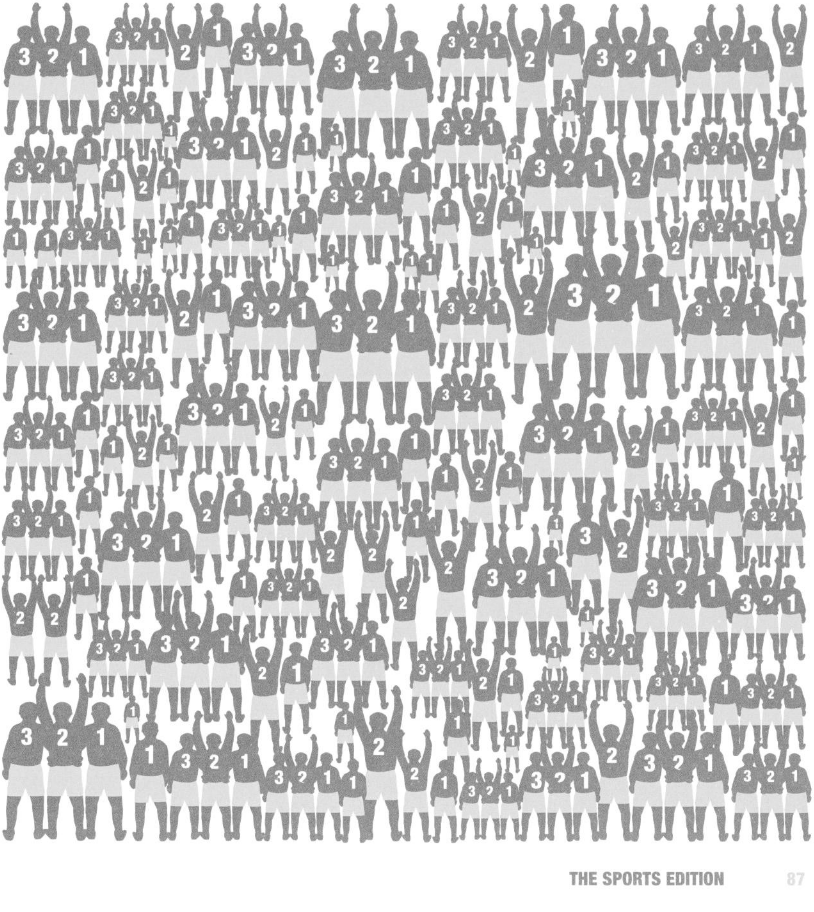

HANDSOMELY TOP
BRITISH MALE – LA 1984
DECATHLON

JEANS ICINESS
BRITISH FEMALE – LONDON 2012
HEPTATHLON

INHALE ACLOUTING
AMERICAN FEMALE – ATHENS 2004
SWIMMING 100 M BACKSTROKE

NANNY JOKES
BRITISH MALE – RIO 2016
TRACK CYCLING INDIVIDUAL SPRINT

BAMBOO RATTLE
ITALIAN MALE – VANCOUVER 2010
SKIING DOWNHILL

VENDSIN ONLY
AMERICAN FEMALE – VANCOUVER 2010
SKIING DOWNHILL

HELPS EACHLIMP
AMERICAN MALE – LONDON 2012
SWIMMING 100 M BUTTERFLY MEN

SNAIL BOUT
JAMAICAN MALE – BEIJING 2008
100 M

ULTRA TAROT
BRITISH FEMALE – RIO 2016
TRACK CYCLING OMNIUM

CLEANLY RESHARPENS FRY
JAMAICAN FEMALE – BEIJING 2008
100 M

S_____ S_____ GLASGOW WARRIORS

S____ S____ WORCESTER WARRIORS

K_____ S_____ GLOUCESTER

R___ P____ NEWPORT DRAGONS

C_____ A___ P____ CARDIFF BLUES

P___ Y S___ SCARLETS

L____ S____ OSPREYS

S___ P___ EXETER CHIEFS

T__ R__ BATH

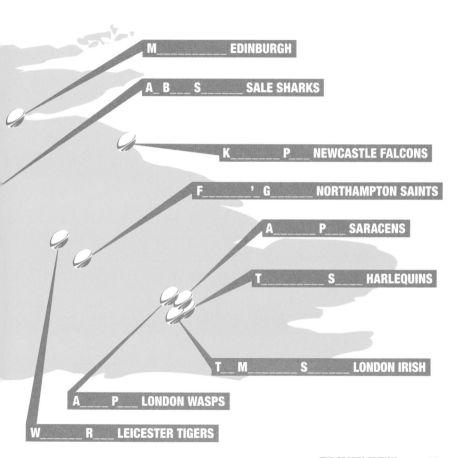

M_____ EDINBURGH

A_ B___ S_____ SALE SHARKS

K_____ P____ NEWCASTLE FALCONS

F_____' G_____ NORTHAMPTON SAINTS

A_____ P____ SARACENS

T_____ S_____ HARLEQUINS

T__ M_____ S_____ LONDON IRISH

A_____ P____ LONDON WASPS

W_____ R____ LEICESTER TIGERS

IN 1985 BORIS BECKER BECAME THE YOUNGEST MALE TO WIN WIMBLEDON – WHAT OTHER FIRSTS DID HIS WIN ACHIEVE?

A) FIRST GERMAN / FIRST LEFT-HANDER

B) FIRST STRAIGHT-SETS WIN / FIRST UNSEEDED

C) FIRST UNSEEDED / FIRST GERMAN

WHICH OF THESE HEAVYWEIGHT BOXING CHAMPIONS RETIRED UNDEFEATED?

A) GEORGE FOREMAN

B) LENNOX LEWIS

C) ROCKY MARCIANO

ADVANTAGE   DIRECT FREE KICK   THROW-IN   OFFSIDE

INDIRECT FREE KICK   SUBSTITUTION   CAUTION

ALL BLACKS
BARBARIANS
ISLANDERS
JAGUARS
LEOPARDS
LES BLEUS
LIONS
PUMAS
SPRINGBOKS
WALLABIES

M	W	A	L	L	A	B	I	E	S
A	N	B	L	I	O	N	S	K	N
L	V	L	C	S	J	X	O	L	A
L	A	E	S	L	A	B	D	E	I
B	F	O	J	A	G	G	H	S	R
L	J	P	K	N	U	S	L	B	A
A	W	A	I	D	A	A	E	L	B
C	R	R	T	E	R	M	Y	E	R
K	P	D	U	R	S	U	X	U	A
S	I	S	O	S	P	P	G	S	B

WHO WAS THE FIRST PERSON TO WIN THE FIFA WORLD CUP BOTH AS A FOOTBALL PLAYER AND A MANAGER?

A) ALF RAMSEY

B) HELMUT SCHÖN

C) MARIO ZAGALLO

**WHO WAS THE FIRST CRICKET PLAYER
TO SCORE A CENTURY AND TAKE
10 WICKETS IN A TEST MATCH?**

A) IMRAN KHAN

B) IAN BOTHAM

C) GARFIELD SOBERS

ANSWERS

P4–5

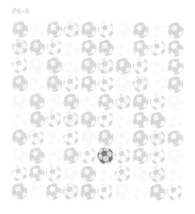

P10–11

```
S F Q U N A H S H M
H O C K E Y S V E T N
D O S A T C A C R E B
Y O F G B B A U R E C
B T B L K B A Q I N Y
B A M N L B S C N C
G L G O L F V K I L
U L R E W Q C E S I
G B A D M I N T O N G
T Y U I O P S Q U G
```

P6 B) POLO P7 B) 155 (FOUL, FREE BALL+ALL REDS+COLOURS)
P8–9

52 THINGS TO DO WHILE YOU POO

P20–21

CELTIC PARK CELTIC

IBROX STADIUM RANGERS

EWOOD PARK BLACKBURN ROVERS

CITY OF MANCHESTER STADIUM MANCHESTER CITY

OLD TRAFFORD MANCHESTER UNITED

GOODISON PARK EVERTON

ANFIELD LIVERPOOL

MOLINEUX WOLVERHAMPTON WANDERERS

THE HAWTHORNS WEST BROMWICH ALBION

LIBERTY STADIUM SWANSEA CITY

CARDIFF CITY STADIUM CARDIFF CITY

ASHTON GATE BRISTOL CITY

ELLAND ROAD LEEDS UNITED

PITTODRIE STADIUM ABERDEEN

TANNADICE PARK DUNDEE UNITED

ST JAMES' PARK NEWCASTLE UNITED

STADIUM OF LIGHT SUNDERLAND

RIVERSIDE STADIUM MIDDLESBROUGH

HILLSBOROUGH STADIUM SHEFFIELD WEDNESDAY

BRAMALL LANE SHEFFIELD UNITED

WHITE HART LANE TOTTENHAM HOTSPUR

UPTON PARK WEST HAM

SELHURST PARK CRYSTAL PALACE

STAMFORD BRIDGE CHELSEA

CRAVEN COTTAGE FULHAM

ASHBURTON GROVE ARSENAL

FILBERT WAY LEICESTER CITY

FRATTON PARK PORTSMOUTH

O: OMAN, L: LAOS, LATVIA, LEBANON, LESOTHO, LIBERIA, LIBYA, LIECHTENSTEIN, LITHUANIA, LUXEMBOURG, Y: YEMEN, M: MACEDONIA, MADAGASCAR, MALAWI, MALAYSIA, MALAYA, MALDIVES, MALI, MALTA, MARSHALL ISLANDS, MAURITANIA, MAURITIUS, MEXICO, FEDERATED STATES OF MICRONESIA, MOLDOVA, MONACO, MONGOLIA, MONTENEGRO, MOROCCO, MOZAMBIQUE, MYANMAR, P: PAKISTAN, PALAU, PALESTINE, PANAMA, PAPUA NEW GUINEA, PARAGUAY, PERU, PHILIPPINES, POLAND, PORTUGAL, PUERTO RICO, I: ICELAND, INDIA, INDONESIA, IRAN, IRAQ, IRELAND, ISRAEL, ITALY C: CAMBODIA, CAMEROON, CANADA, CAPE VERDE, CAYMAN ISLANDS, CENTRAL AFRICAN REPUBLIC, CHAD, CHILE, CHINA, CHINESE TAIPEI, S: SAINT KITTS AND NEVIS, SAINT LUCIA, SAINT VINCENT AND THE GRENADINES, SAMOA, SAN MARINO, SÃO TOMÉ AND PRÍNCIPE, SAUDI ARABIA, SENEGA, SERBIA, SEYCHELLES, SIERRA LEONE, SINGAPORE, SLOVAKIA, SLOVENIA, SOLOMON ISLANDS, SOMALIA, SOUTH AFRICA, SPAIN, SRI LANKA, SUDAN, SOUTH SUDAN, SURINAME, SWAZILAND, SWEDEN, SWITZERLAND, SYRIA.

52 THINGS TO DO WHILE YOU POO

OUT NO BALL BYE BOUNDARY 6 NEW BALL WIDE LEG-BYE SHORT RUN

THE SPORTS EDITION 103

52 THINGS TO DO WHILE YOU POO

PENALTY   FREE KICK   KNOCK ON   TRY   FORWARD PASS   OBSTRUCTION   BALL NOT RELEASED   LINE-OUT THROW NOT STRAIGHT

P46–47

DONALD BRADMAN	GARY SOBERS	VIVIAN RICHARDS
AUSTRALIAN BATSMAN	WEST INDIAN ALL-ROUNDER	WEST INDIAN BATSMAN

IMRAN KHAN	IAN BOTHAM	DENNIS LILLEE
PAKISTANI ALL-ROUNDER	ENGLISH ALL-ROUNDER	AUSTRALIAN FAST BOWLER

JACQUES KALLIS	JAVED MIANDAD	SHANE WARNE
SOUTH AFRICAN ALL-ROUNDER	PAKISTANI BATSMAN	AUSTRALIAN SPIN BOWLER

WASIM AKRAM	BRIAN LARA	RICKY PONTING
PAKISTANI ALL-ROUNDER	WEST INDIAN BATSMAN	AUSTRALIAN BATSMAN

P50 B) DUBLIN UNI FC P51 C) PAPUA NEW GUINEA
P52 THE LETTER 'O' (SORRY!)
P53

P48–49

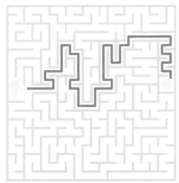

52 THINGS TO DO WHILE YOU POO

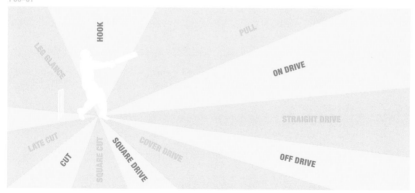

P66 B) 10 P67 A) SCOTLAND
P68–69

P70 A) 11 HOURS AND 5 MINUTES
P71 C) BOTH PAIRS WERE IDENTICAL TWINS
P72–73

P74 SPAIN P75 C) CHUKKAS
P76–77

COVENTRY CITY
FA CUP
WINNERS 1987

ABERDEEN
UEFA CUP
WINNERS 1983

WEST GERMANY
WORLD CUP
WINNERS 1990

WERDER BREMEN
UEFA CUP
WINNERS 1992

TOTTENHAM HOTSPUR
FA CUP
WINNERS 1967

INTER MILAN
COPPA ITALIA
WINNERS 2011

IVORY COAST
AFRICA CUP OF NATIONS
WINNERS 1992

ATLETICO MADRID
COPA DEL REY
WINNERS 2013

DUNDEE UNITED
SCOTTISH CUP
WINNERS 2010

ARGENTINA
WORLD CUP
WINNERS 1986

SWANSEA CITY
WELSH CUP
WINNERS 1991

WIGAN ATHLETIC
FA CUP
WINNERS 2013

P88–89

DALEY THOMPSON
BRITISH MALE – LA 1984
DECATHLON

JESSICA ENNIS
BRITISH FEMALE – LONDON 2012
HEPTATHLON

LINDSEY VONN
AMERICAN FEMALE – VANCOUVER 2010
SKIING DOWNHILL

MICHAEL PHELPS
AMERICAN MALE – LONDON 2012
SWIMMING 100 M BUTTERFLY/200 M

NATALIE COUGHLIN
AMERICAN FEMALE – ATHENS 2004
SWIMMING 100 M BACKSTROKE

USAIN BOLT
JAMAICAN MALE – BEIJING 2008
100 M

JASON KENNY
BRITISH MALE – RIO 2016
TRACK CYCLING INDIVIDUAL SPRINT

ALBERTO TOMBA
ITALIAN MALE – VANCOUVER 2010
SKIING DOWNHILL

LAURA TROTT
BRITISH FEMALE – RIO 2016
TRACK CYCLING OMNIUM

SHELLY-ANN FRASER-PRYCE
JAMAICAN FEMALE – BEIJING 2008
100 M

P90–91

SCOTSTOUN STADIUM GLASGOW WARRIORS

MURRAYFIELD EDINBURGH

SIXWAYS STADIUM WORCESTER WARRIORS

AJ BELL STADIUM SALE SHARKS

KINGSHOLM STADIUM GLOUCESTER

KINGSTON PARK NEWCASTLE FALCONS

RODNEY PARADE NEWPORT DRAGONS

FRANKLIN'S GARDENS NORTHAMPTON SAINTS

ALLIANZ PARK SARACENS

CARDIFF ARMS PARK CARDIFF BLUES

TWICKENHAM STOOP HARLEQUINS

PARC Y SCARLETS SCARLETS

LIBERTY STADIUM OSPREYS

THE MADEJSKI STADIUM LONDON IRISH

ADAMS PARK LONDON WASPS

SANDY PARK EXETER CHIEFS

THE REC BATH

WELFORD ROAD LEICESTER TIGERS

DIRECT FREE KICK   INDIRECT FREE KICK   ADVANTAGE   CAUTION   THROW-IN   SUBSTITUTION   OFFSIDE

P96–97   P98 **C) MARIO ZAGALLO** P99 **B) IAN BOTHAM**

IF YOU'RE INTERESTED IN FINDING OUT MORE
ABOUT OUR BOOKS, FIND US ON FACEBOOK
AT SUMMERSDALE PUBLISHERS AND FOLLOW
US ON TWITTER AT @SUMMERSDALE.

WWW.SUMMERSDALE.COM